CW00553576

The
History
of Wales in
Twelve Poems

I'm teulu a'm ffrindiau oll, sy ac a fu.
And in memory of Neil Reeve (1953–2018).

The
History of Wales in Twelve Poems

M. WYNN THOMAS
Illustrations by Ruth Jên Evans

University of Wales Press
2021

www.uwp.co.uk

British Library CIP Data

A catalogue record for this book is available from the British Library.

ISBN   978-1-78683-766-0
eISBN   978-1-78683-767-7

The right of M. Wynn Thomas to be identified as author of this
work has been asserted in accordance with sections 77 and 79
of the Copyright, Designs and Patents Act 1988.

For the University of Wales Press:
Sarah Lewis (Commissioning); Olwen Fowler (Design);
Siân Chapman (Production); Dafydd Jones (Editorial).
Printed by CPI Antony Rowe, Melksham.

The publisher acknowledges the financial support
of the Books Council of Wales.

Powerful nations have great poets;
small nations have tragic poets.
They do our dying for us, whisper the
powerful nations, sensing the insecurity
of their power. In this way we produce
great poets, whisper the small nations.

George Szirtes

Contents

Acknowledgements

Aneirin, 'Y Gododdin', Thomas Parry (ed.), *Oxford Book of Welsh Verse* (Oxford: Oxford University Press, 1998), pp. 1–2; trans. M. Wynn Thomas.

Anon., 'Pais Dinogad', Thomas Parry (ed.), *Oxford Book of Welsh Verse* (Oxford: Oxford University Press, 1998), pp. 7–8; trans. Tony Conran, *Welsh Verse* (Bridgend: Seren Books, 2003), p. 117.

Anon., 'Stafell Gynddylan', Thomas Parry (ed.), *Oxford Book of Welsh Verse* (Oxford: Oxford University Press, 1998), p. 12; 'Cynddylan's Hall', trans. Tony Conran, *Welsh Verse* (Bridgend: Seren Books, 2003), p. 12.

Gruffydd ab yr Ynad Coch, 'Marwnad Llywelyn ap Gruffudd', Thomas Parry (ed.), *Oxford Book of Welsh Verse* (Oxford: Oxford University Press, 1998), pp. 47–8; 'Elegy for Llywelyn ap Gruffydd', trans. Tony Conran, *Welsh Verse* (Bridgend: Seren Books, 2003), p. 163.

Dafydd ap Gwilym, 'Trafferth mewn Tafarn', *dafyddapgwilym.net*; trans. M. Wynn Thomas.

Henry Vaughan, 'The World', L. C. Martin (ed.), *Henry Vaughan, Poetry and Prose* (London: Oxford University Press, 1963), pp. 299–301.

Anon., 'Hen Benillion', T. H. Parry-Williams (ed.), *Hen Benillion* (Llandysul: Gwasg Gomer, 2010), pp. 28–9; 'Harp stanzas', trans. Glyn Jones, *A People's Poetry: Hen Benillion* (Bridgend: Seren Books, 1997), pp. 160–1.

Ann Griffiths, 'Wele'n sefyll rhwng y myrtwydd'; 'See – there stands', trans. Joseph P. Clancy, *Other Words: Essays, Poetry and Translation* (Cardiff: University of Wales Press, 1999), p. 27.

Gwenallt, 'Y Meirwon', Christine James (ed.), *Cerddi Gwenallt: Y Casgliad Cyflawn* (Llandysul: Gwasg Gomer, 2001), pp. 139–40; 'The Dead', trans. Tony Conran, *Welsh Verse* (Bridgend: Seren Books, 2003), p. 163.

Dylan Thomas, 'Fern Hill', Walford Davies and Ralph Maud (eds), *Dylan Thomas: Collected Poems, 1934–1953* (London: Dent, 1988), pp. 134–5. © 1945 by the Trustees for the Copyrights of Dylan Thomas. Reprinted by permission of New Directions Publishing Corp. and David Higham Associates.

Gillian Clarke, 'Blodeuwedd', *Collected Poems* (Manchester: Carcanet, 1992), pp. 69–70.

Menna Elfyn, 'Siapau o Gymru'/ 'The Shapes She Makes' (trans. Elin ap Hywel), *Eucalyptus* (Llandysul: Gomer, 1995), pp. 98–101.

Preface

Having, like their cousins the Irish, a long, ancient taproot in a Celtic culture, the Welsh have always revered the number three. From the ancient Tribannau and Trioedd Ynys Prydain, to the three feathers in the badge of the medieval Prince of Wales, to the persistence to this day of the popular saying 'Tri chynnig i Gymro' (Three tries for a Welshman), the three has been accorded mystic status. And in modern times, even the phrase 'three tries' has taken on a different meaning, as the Welsh rugby team have a distinguished record of winning the premier home nations title of the Triple Crown. With all of this in mind, let me conform to established cultural practice and offer three reasons for writing this book.

First, there is the plight of the Invisible Nation. When, half a century ago, I read Ralph Ellison's classic novel *Invisible Man* (before discovering it had been begun when he was a GI in Swansea), what struck me even beyond its unforgettable account of the complex fate of being an African-American was that the narrative had unexpectedly offered me a fascinating glimpse of myself. I was of course fully aware that there was not the slightest comparison between my own sorry plight and the immense tragedy of Ellison and his people, but I still couldn't help reflecting that I too knew what it was to be invisible. From an early age, I had intuited that the Welsh were not only invisible to the world at large, but that they were also, tragically, mostly invisible even to themselves. That invisibility – deriving as it obviously does from long centuries of subordination, marginalisation, and assimilation – has continued to haunt and to frustrate me. This brief history is therefore an attempt to make my Wales just a little easier to see.

As for the second reason for writing, it can best be expressed through the story of Tinker Bell. She, it will be remembered, is the fey fairy in J. M. Barrie's *Peter Pan*. Yes, she can be mischievous, wilful, even spiteful, but in the end she is a deeply poignant creation. Her very existence, signified by the frail glow of light she emits, is entirely dependent on there being children enough who stubbornly continue, even in the face all the scoffing scepticism of the modern world of adult experience, to believe in fairies. And as the narrative proceeds to its conclusion, so does Tinker Bell's fragile gleam grow ever fainter, extinguished at last in the darkness of her total extinction.

The Welsh, I have long felt, are not only an invisible people, they are a Tinker Bell of a people. For almost as long as the history of Wales itself, theirs has had to be a survivor culture's precarious, conditional, identity. Devoid of the robust supporting mechanism of an established state, and lacking the complex infrastructure necessary to ensure the safe transmission of a national culture, the Welsh have had no choice but to exist by effortfully *choosing* to do so and by constantly improvising strategies of self-renewal. In no other instance than theirs has Renan's famous description of nationhood as a daily plebiscite seemed more apt. This mini-history is therefore an attempt to ensure that the light of this Tinkerbell people continues to burn for a short while longer, at least.

And thirdly? Well, it concerns the poets. Wales is often recognised as the home of significant singers, from stars of popular culture such as Shirley Bassey, Tom Jones and Katherine Jenkins to giants of the operatic stage, such as Bryn Terfel, Gwyneth Jones, Geraint Evans and Rebecca Evans. Welsh actors likewise enjoy a good reputation – for their acting, if not always for their lifestyles – witness Richard Burton, Anthony Hopkins, Siân Phillips, Michael Sheen and Catherine Zeta Jones.

But what of the poets of Wales? True, the Welsh national anthem ('Hen Wlad fy Nhadau'/'Land of my Fathers') proudly trumpets Wales to be 'gwlad beirdd a chantorion' (a land of poets and singers). And, oh dear me, yes, there is the evergreen Dylan Thomas. But is there life beyond Dylan? Has there ever been?

The answer is a resounding yes, and yes again. Such is the depth and pedigree of Welsh poetry that it is even questionable whether Dylan Thomas should be treated as the pre-eminent figure in a millennium and a half of tradition.

The great Native American writer N. Scott Momaday has written: 'We are what we imagine. Our very existence consists in the imagination of ourselves. The greatest tragedy that can befall us is to go unimagined.' It is the poets of Wales, above all, who have carried that burden of imagining a nation down the many centuries.

This volume, therefore, sets out to place the poets of Wales at the very forefront of Welsh history. It is a position they deserve, by virtue not only of their quality but of the crucial role they have always played in the maintenance of a Welsh identity. Today, poetry in Wales, as throughout the western world, is socially marginalised, and no more than a minority interest. Yet still, important aspects of contemporary Welsh anglophone identity are perilously freighted by the popular image of Dylan Thomas's stormy career and more accessible works.

But there is one important caveat that needs adding in this connection. There is no intention here to construct an anthology of the greatest poetry of Wales. Rather, the poems included in this rapid overview of 1,500 years of history have been selected primarily for their functional value: they simply offer the reader what I hope is an interesting way into the social, political and cultural history of the different phases of the long and varied Welsh past.

Finally, my warmest thanks to my good friends Professors Kirsti Bohata, Ceri Davies, Menna Elfyn and Dafydd Johnston for casting an eye over previous versions of this text, and offering valuable corrections and improvements. Diolch o galon ichi i gyd am eich trafferth.

M. Wynn Thomas

Y Gododdin

seventh century

Gwŷr a aeth Gatraeth oedd ffraeth eu llu;
Glasfedd eu hancwyn, a gwenwyn fu.
Trichant trwy beiriant yn catáu –
A gwedi elwch tawelwch fu.
Cyd elwynt lannau i benydu,
Dadl diau angau i eu treiddu …

O freithell Gatraeth pan adroddir,
Maon dychiorant; eu hoed bu hir.
Edyrn diedyrn amgyn' dir
Â meibion Godebog, gwerin enwir.
Dyfforthynt lynwysawr gelorawr hir.
Bu tru o dynghedfen, angen gywir,
A dyngwyd i Dudfwlch a Chyfwlch Hir.
Cyd yfem fedd gloyw wrth leu babir,
Cyd fai da ei flas, ei gas bu hir.

Catraeth-bent went a voluble host.
Three hundred packed in close array.
Din of feast;   then
                                    Silence.
Due penance done in myriad churches,
Yet stone-deaf death riddled them through …

Tales come from Catraeth tell
How heroes fell, were mourned long.
Fierce land-protectors,
Sons of Godebog, true to the end.
Bodies stretched on blood-soaked biers,
Doomed to face the wretched reckoning
Decreed to Tudfwlch and Cyfwlch Hir.
Glow of wine in candle flame,
Sweet the taste, the aftertaste bitter.

This famous seventh-century work by Aneirin is one of the very earliest poems in Welsh to have survived, and it shows how Welsh poetry began to take distinctive shape. One of its lines in particular has lingered in the collective mind for a millennium and a half: 'Ac wedi elwch tawelwch fu.' 'Elwch' is 'feasting', 'tawelwch' is 'silence': the raw, brutal juxtaposition of the two simple words sends a shiver down the mind's spine; while the tie of rhyme makes the fateful link between the two inexorable. Moreover 'tawelwch', 'silence', is actually composed of 'taw' (to put an end to') and 'elwch' ('feasting').

Such a memorable composition makes clear the part poetry began to play in the fashioning of a new language – 'Welsh' – out of a mixture of the original Celtic tongue and elements from the Latin of the Roman conquerors. The making of this new language was also the making of a new people. In early Welsh the word 'iaith' stood both for a language and for the people who spoke it. The tribal poets ('bards') played an important role in all these developments and were accordingly granted a highly respected place in the social structure of the day. They were the custodians of tradition, lore and tribal 'history', and they sang the praises of the heroes of a warrior society.

Following the withdrawal of most Roman troops with Macsen Wledig (Magnus Maximus, 383 CE), the speakers of this new language were scattered across much of mainland Britain. But they came increasingly under attack from bands of foreign marauders from the Continent. The Catraeth poem tells the story of one such native group's brave and epic attempt to fend off Germanic invaders at Catraeth (Catterick). It speaks of a tiny warrior band that was feted and feasted for a whole year before being sent to heroic annihilation in battle with a much greater enemy force.

That band actually started out on its futile quest not from Wales but from the lowlands of Scotland. The fate that befell it foreshadows that of many others of the native

Britons the length and breadth of the island who tried to defend their territories. The invaders steadily prevailed, driving wedges that left the natives isolated from each other until eventually the remnants of indigenous society were confined to small marginal areas such as modern Cumbria (which comes from the same root as 'Cymru') and Cornwall. From there a small group fled further to Brittany, which became known as 'Little Britain' to distinguish it from 'Great Britain' – in origin the term had nothing to do with a global British Empire. But, of course, above all they retreated to Wales.

There the people came to call their land self-protectively 'Cymru', and themselves first 'Brythoniaid' (Britons) and then 'Cymry' ('comrades'), although the invaders – mostly of Saxon origin – referred to them dismissively as 'Welsh' (a foreign, Romanised people). With the passing of the

centuries, their relations with their neighbours took the form not only of sporadic confrontation but of judicious intermarriages, diplomatic alliances and cultural exchanges. Coastal regions were particularly important areas of encounter – sea voyaging was after all much the easiest mode of travel, and made possible significant incursions and extensive settlements from Ireland and also by Viking invaders.

The names of several of the most prominent 'tribal' warlords of the period have come down to us through legend (e.g. Gwrtheyrn/ Vortigern; Arthur). The names given to some of the more powerful and stable of their often fluid regional societies also remain in present-day vocabulary, as in Dyfed, Gwynedd and Powys. Some of these regional overlords even proved sufficiently powerful to extend their sovereignty over virtually the entire area of the country and could thus reasonably claim to be princes of the whole of Wales, a prominent example being Rhodri Mawr in the ninth century.

These Romano-British peoples who were in the process of becoming collectively known as 'the Welsh' had become Christianised before the departure of the Roman legions, and were thereafter to remain bound closely to that religion first through their own holy-men (the 'Celtic saints', most famously David) and then by being (reluctantly at first) plugged in, through their monks and clergy, to the Europe-wide system of the Catholic religious establishment. Wales duly developed its own great monastic centres of learning at Llanilltud Fawr (Llantwit Major, where the earliest

Celtic saints of Ireland were educated), Llandeilo Fawr and Llanbadarn.

From the manuscripts that were eventually produced there, as later in the Norman monasteries, we glean many of the uncertain 'facts' that allow us glimpses of early Welsh 'history'. Mention is made for instance of Cunedda, a powerful warlord from lowland Scotland, reputed to have established a sixth-century dynasty in Gwynedd, some members of which went on to create their own power bases in areas subsequently named after them – Ceredig(ion), Meirion(nydd), etc. And we also hear of Gwrtheyrn (Vortigern), the ruler credited with the disastrous decision to invite mercenary Saxon bands over from the Continent to bolster-up his power.

As the centuries passed, and a series of ever more powerful and stable regional 'kingdoms' rose and fell the far side of the boundary Dyke that had been established, with Welsh co-operation, by Offa king of Mercia, the Welsh peoples responded by variously resisting, adapting and bending the knee to superior power in order carefully to protect what remained to them of 'independence' and self-rule. It was a mixed policy that allowed for important cultural exchanges: for instance, the celebrated code of laws constructed in Dyfed (south-west Wales) by Hywel Dda (Hywel the Good), a particularly enlightened tenth-century ruler of the large part of Wales, owed much to his connections with Wessex as well as to his familiarity with continental precedents.

ANON.

Pais Dinogad

seventh century

Pais Dinogad, fraith fraith,
O grwyn balaod ban wraith:
Chwid, chwid, chwidogaith,
Gochanwn, gochenyn' wythgaith.
Pan elai dy dad di i heliaw,
Llath ar ei ysgwydd, llory yn ei law,
Ef gelwi gŵn gogyhwg –
'Giff gaff; daly, daly, dwg, dwg.'
Ef lleddi bysg yng nghorwg
Mal ban lladd llew llywiwg
Pan elai dy dad di i fynydd,
Dyddygai ef pen iwrch, pen gwythwch, pen hydd,
Pen grugiar fraith o fynydd,
Pen pysg o Raeadr Derwennydd.
O'r sawl yd gyrhaeddai dy dad di â'i gigwain
O wythwch a llewyn a llwynain
Nid angai oll ni fai oradain.

Dinogad's smock is pied, pied –
Made it out of marten hide.
Whit, whit, whistle along,
Eight slaves with you sing the song.

When your dad went to hunt,
Spear on his shoulder, cudgel in hand,
He called his quick dogs, 'Giff, you wretch,
Gaff, catch her, catch her, fetch, fetch!'

From a coracle he'd spear
Fish as a lion strikes a deer,
When your dad went to the crag
He brought down roebuck, boar and stag,
Speckled grouse from the mountain tall,
Fish from Derwent waterfall.

Whatever your dad found with his spear,
Boar or wild cat, fox or deer,
Unless it flew, would never get clear.

This enchanting lullaby with its tender domestic setting dates back possibly to the seventh century. It delightfully captures a mother (perhaps) 'bigging up' her man, the sleeping baby's father, and it evokes an everyday masculine world of fishing, hunt and chase. It therefore briefly grants us – just like an exquisite miniature in a great medieval Books of Hours – a very rare intimate glimpse into the ordinary life of the time. And in being sung by a woman, this loving cradle song briefly breaks the terrible eternal silence to which the poor anonymous masses of this era have otherwise been condemned by history. This fragment, therefore, brings to our modern attention the plight of this vast population of the unheard – the girls, the women, the babies, the children, the physically and mentally impaired, the old and the infirm; all the callously casual casualties of conflict; and all members of the huge underclass of serf and slave labour upon which a warrior society in reality totally depended for basic sustenance, for all its macho heroics and cult of alpha-male heroes.

A few other poems from this era also allow us parallel glimpses into a mysterious underworld of experience otherwise forbidden to us. There is the remarkable legend of the distracted Myrddin Wyllt, for example. He was driven so mad by the carnage he witnessed at Arfderydd that he took refuge in a dense forest with only a pig for company and an apple tree for comfort. His story surely offers us a remarkable early case-study of 'post-traumatic stress disorder'. The speaker in 'Claf Abercuawg' (ninth or tenth century) is a former warrior now relegated to the sidelines and a devastating uselessness by his leprosy; and the poetic cycle attributed to Llywarch Hen (ninth or tenth century) vividly records the crisis of masculinity experienced by an ageing, hunchbacked warrior, whose powerlessness is imaged, with phallic suggestiveness, by the substitution of a crutch for a spear. In a desperate attempt to recover his former prowess vicariously through his sons, he goads all twenty-four of them to their death, leaving the old man desolate and devastated by guilt.

This bleak, Freudian family saga seems to encapsulate the crisis at the centre of late-heroic society, as the old warrior code, based on the individual prowess still defiantly celebrated in the face of catastrophic defeat in the Catraeth poem, proved disastrously inadequate to a new world. There, as the millennium approached, the Welsh peoples were increasingly faced by foes of overwhelming might. The greatest of these to emerge at the beginning of the second millennium were of course the Normans – but even before them, the Saxons-turned-English had grown so powerful by the tenth century that the poem *Armes Prydein* fantasises a great alliance not only of all the Celtic peoples of the Isles, but also including the Danes, to expel the English and drive them once and for all beyond the sea. While such an alliance remained in the realms of fantasy, a real alliance of the day – in the form of marriage between a Welsh leader and a Danish princess from Dublin –

led to the tenth-century creation in Gwynedd, under their son Gruffudd ap Cynan, of a powerful political dynasty that would dominate Wales for the last two centuries of native rule.

ANON.

Stafell Gynddylan

ninth or tenth century

Stafell Gynddylan ys tywyll heno,
    Heb dân, heb wely;
  Wylaf wers, tawaf wedy.

Stafell Gynddylan ys tywyll heno,
    Heb dân, heb gannwyll;
  Namyn Duw pwy a'm dyry pwyll? ....

Stafell Gynddylan ys tywyll heno,
    Heb dân, heb gerddau;
  Dygystudd deurudd dagrau.

Stafell Gynddylan, a'm gwân ei gweled
    Heb döed, heb dân;
  Marw fy nglyw, byw fy hunan.

Stafell Gynddylan, a'm erwan pob awr
    Gwedi mawr ymgyfrdan
  A welais ar dy bentan.

Dark is Cynddylan's hall tonight
　　With no fire, no bed.
　I weep awhile, then am silent.

Dark is Cynddylan's hall tonight
　　With no fire, no candle.
　Save God, who'll keep me sane? ...

Dark is Cynddylan's hall tonight
　　With no fire, no songs.
　My cheek's worn out with tears.

It wounds me to see Cynddylan's hall
　　With no roof, no fire,
　Dead is my lord; I yet live …

Hour upon hour, Cynddylan's hall wounds me
　　After the great conversing
　That I watched on your hearth.

Although it was 1282 before the end of that native world came, the devastation that followed as the old order finally collapsed had, in a way, been symbolically anticipated in a great ninth-century elegy. It was sung by an imaginary character called Heledd, who was mourning the death of her whole family and the total destruction of their ruling house in the borderlands of Powys. So here again we briefly and very unusually glimpse the grim fate of a warrior society as viewed through the eyes not of one of its victors but of one of its most vulnerable victims, a totally defenceless woman.

It is another reminder of the bloodshed that went into the fashioning and defending of these early transient societies, particularly as they came under ever-increasing pressure from the growing powers beyond the Dyke, where the various regions steadily consolidated into a single kingdom eventually to be known as England. When, therefore, we compile a roster of the names of notable leaders and warlords from shortly before and after the millennium – Rhodri Mawr, Hywel Dda, Gruffudd ap Llywelyn, Gruffudd ap Cynan, Owain Gwynedd,

Llywelyn Fawr, etc. – we are implicitly acknowledging their remarkable (and no doubt ruthless) skills of surviving and even flourishing under extremely testing conditions. Hence the established practice of dignifying them with the honorific titles of 'King' and 'Prince'.

In the 'Age of the Princes' the court poets (such as Cynddelw Brydydd Mawr) – whose poetry had become rigorously systematised, learned, and ornately garnished with linguistic anachronisms – continued to perform an invaluable service, and so enjoyed enormous prestige. The arrival of the Normans on the far shores of England, however, dramatically and irrevocably altered the balance of power. They soon established an impregnable power base on the Welsh borders, after which the south of Wales (most notably the future Cardiganshire, Pembrokeshire, Glamorganshire and Breconshire) was quickly penetrated and subjugated piecemeal by means of a string of castles serving to protect the mighty occupying force. So powerful were the great Lords of the Welsh March that the allegiance they owed to whichever Anglo-Norman king was currently in power and sporadically intervened grew decidedly tenuous.

The immensely powerful religious arm of the Norman conquest was the Catholic Church and its many monastic orders. New and increasingly splendid churches, reinforced by a tiny handful of impressive cathedrals, were established in Wales as instruments of social control, eventually triggering a power struggle for supremacy between St Davids and distant Canterbury.

One of the early bishops of the new foundation was Geoffrey of Monmouth, the Cambro-Norman of Breton descent, whose *Historia Regum Brittanniae* (1136) was to prove an instant European sensation.

Geoffrey not only popularised the aggrandising myth that Britain had been founded by Brutus, a refugee from Troy, but also effectively invented a remarkable superhero of early British ('Welsh') resistance named 'Arthur', whose true contemporary descendants were the Anglo-Normans (and hence subsequently the 'English'). His fantastic fabrication immediately went viral, and the cult of Arthur – probably originating from Welsh legendary sources but now embellished with all the trappings of courtly romance and with a Round Table thrown in to complete the Cecil B. DeMille effect – spread like wildfire right across the Continent. But as if in pre-emptive anticipation of this daylight robbery of its native lore, Welsh society had taken the precaution of committing to paper that wondrous, fertile compilation of ancient tales eventually to be known as *The Mabinogion*.

Effective control of the upland areas of the north, most particularly of Gwynedd, proved to be much more difficult for the Normans. For some two centuries of a protracted end-game, that mountainous area of north-west Wales produced a succession of ingenious native leaders who managed to protect their societies by alternately counterattacking to recover lands lost to the Normans, and (somewhat deviously) compromising. The greatest of these leaders was Llywelyn ap Iorwerth (Llywelyn Fawr/

the Great), the late twelfth-century ruler of Gwynedd and effective prince of native Wales with whom first King John and then Henry III had to come to terms. Significant parts even of the south-west of Wales were recovered and united under the remarkable mid-twelfth-century leadership of the cultured Arglwydd Rhys (the Lord Rhys of Dinefwr), with whom the Normans eventually made peace, formally recognising him as a local justiciary of their system. It was also Rhys who was indirectly responsible for the departure from Pembrokeshire of a Cambro-Norman force that invaded and fatefully conquered the Irish of Leinster.

But catastrophe for the native cause finally came in 1282, when Llywelyn ap Gruffudd (Llywelyn ein Llyw Olaf), the last native 'prince' of Wales, buoyed up by several decades of successful campaigning against the English crown, overstretched himself and fatally miscalculated. During his reign, he established a sophisticated polity with the potential of developing into a full-blown 'state' apparatus, and Caerphilly castle still remains, in its defensive immensity, to testify in stone to the terror Llywelyn could arouse in even the most powerful Marcher lords. But having had the misfortune to cross the grim implacable will of Edward I, a hammerer of the Welsh before he proved such for the Scots, Llywelyn's downfall was inevitable. His ignominious death at Cilmeri, west of Builth, followed by the display of his severed head at the Tower of London, brought an end to what little by then remained of Welsh 'independence'.

As for Edward I, he lost no time in stamping his authority once and for all on what was left of troublesome Wales, establishing castles of previously unimaginable scale and grandeur – later to be called 'the most magnificent badge of our subjection'. These were built at such key locations as Conway, Harlech, Beaumaris and Caernarfon, where the great fortress was consciously based on a model imported from Constantinople to signify the return of Empire to Wales. And it was at Caernarfon that Edward's son was born, later to be publicly pronounced the new Prince of Wales, thus guaranteeing Welsh revenues for the English crown.

Marwnad Llywelyn ap Gruffudd

Elegy for Llywelyn ap Gruffudd

thirteenth century

Oerfalawg calon dan fron o fraw,
Rhewydd fal crinwydd y sy'n crinaw.
Poni welwch chwi hynt y gwynt a'r glaw?
Poni welwch chwi'r deri yn ymdaraw?
Poni welwch chwi'r môr yn meirwinaw'r tir
Poni welwch chwi'r gwir yn ymgweiriaw?
Poni welwch chwi'r haul yn hwylaw'r awyr?
Poni welwch chwi'r sŷr wedi'r syrthiaw?
Pani chredwch chwi i Dduw, ddyniadon ynfyd?
Pani welwch chwi'r byd wedi'r bydiaw?
Och hyd atat Ti, Dduw, na ddaw môr dros dir!
Pa beth y'n gedir i ohiriaw?
Nid oes le y cyrcher rhag carchar braw,
Nid oes le y trigier: och o'r trigiaw!

The heart's gone cold, under a breast of fear;
Lust shrivels like dried brushwood.
See you not the way of the wind and the rain?
See you not oaktrees buffet together?
See you not the sea stinging the land?
See you not truth in travail?
See you not the sun hurtling through the sky,
And that the stars are fallen?
Do you not believe God, demented mortals?
Do you not see the whole world's danger?
Why, O my God, does the sea not cover the land?
Why are we left to linger?
There is no refuge from imprisoning fear,
And nowhere to bide – O such abiding!

Llywelyn's death on the banks of the Irfon at Cilmeri was more than the death of a 'Prince': it was the end of a world. Or rather, the end of the world – the only world that Gruffudd ab yr Ynad Coch and his bardic kind had ever known or could possibly imagine. There were no longer any powerful native leaders to hold court and to nurture those arch-flatterers, their pet poets. There was no longer an indigenous aristocratic elite to cause trouble – those who remained of this class quietly subsided into lower and more modest status or hastily joined the ranks of the occupiers. As for the distinctive native system of decentralised government, observing the Welsh laws of Hywel Dda and based on extensive family ties that had divided the country up into such small units as the 'cantrefi', it continued for a while to be treated as valid.

But it was steadily replaced by the centralised structure of Anglo-Norman rule defined in the Statute of Rhuddlan (1284). Insisting on imposing the foreign legal system of England, this introduced a shire structure, with sheriffs and feudal courts. Recognising the shape of things to come, some of the Welsh duly began to help administer this new system. They also began to enrol in the ranks of the continental armies of the Anglo-Norman kings, and indeed of their continental enemies, in the process gaining notoriety for indiscipline.

While the conquest of Wales was now effectively complete, the Normans were at first disinclined to push their luck too far, granting the native people a fig-leaf of self-respect and of cultural 'freedom' while occupying the commanding heights of all the key sectors of government, law, administration, commerce and religion. The Welsh were excluded from the fortified trading posts their conquerors created – the walled towns of foreign settlement that lurked in the protective lee of the castles that were strategically situated to discourage rebellion and granted privileged licence to trade and to control their own affairs. There were Anglo-Norman laws too that discriminated against the natives in favour of the settlers, and the resentments that ensued helped stimulate periodic native rebellions. As Welsh names had been important indicators of pedigree, and therefore of status, they were gradually shorn of presumption, becoming anglicised so that ap Hywel became Powell, ap Henry = Penry, ap Rhys = Prys, Ifan = Evans, Dafydd = Davies, and so on and so forth. And with the passage of time, the Anglo-Normans steadily strengthened their grip, so that such leaders as remained to the Welsh either served loyally in the wars of English kings or – as in the legendary case of 'Owain Lawgoch' – served as mercenaries in the armies of great continental figures such as the French kings.

The mixed results of such a settlement were nowhere more vividly evident than in the case of the Tudor family of Penmynydd on Anglesey. Long after they had removed themselves from Wales and become thoroughly assimilated into Anglo-French polity, they retained sufficient cultural memory of legendary Welsh history to use the desperate old Welsh compensatory fantasies of recovering the throne of the whole Island of Britain to devastating dynastic advantage. This began with Henry Tudor's landfall at Milford Haven in August 1485, which led to his Welsh-assisted victory at the battle of Bosworth. After his crowning as Henry VII, many of the leaders of Welsh society made unseemly haste to the flourishing court of the 'Welsh' Tudors. A startling number of the notables of later Tudor and Elizabethan England were, accordingly, of Welsh descent – the poets George Herbert and John Donne (of rumoured descent from the Dwnns of Kidwelly); the great 'magus' John Dee; the sinister Lord Cecil (of the Welsh Sisyll family) and several others. (Dee it was who coined the term 'British Empire', where 'British' meant 'Ancient British', on the convenient and fanciful supposition that America had been discovered by the twelfth-century Prince Madoc of Gwynedd.) Thus did London embark on its long modern history as the true 'capital' of Wales, the irresistible honeypot of talent. It was a development that proved to be of immense advantage and disadvantage to Wales.

Trafferth mewn Tafarn

Tavern Trouble

fourteenth century

Deuthum i ddinas dethol
A'm hardd wreang i'm hôl.
Cain hoywdraul, lle cwyn hydrum,
Cymryd, balch o febyd fûm,
Llety, urddedig ddigawn,
Cyffredin, a gwin a gawn.
Canfod rhiain addfeindeg
Yn y tŷ, f'un enaid teg.
Bwrw yn llwyr, liw haul dwyrain,
Fy mryd ar wyn fy myd main,
Prynu rhost, nid er bostiaw,
A gwin drud, mi a gwen draw …

Gwedy cysgu, tru tremyn,
O bawb onid mi a bun,
Ceisiais yn hyfedr fedru
Ar wely'r ferch, alar fu.
Cefais, pan soniais yna,
Gwymp dig, nid oedd gampau da.
Briwais, ni neidiais yn iach,
Y grimog, a gwae'r omach,
Wrth ystlys, ar waith ostler,
Ystôl groch ffôl, goruwch ffêr.
Trewais, drwg fydd tra awydd,
Lle y'm rhoed, heb un llam rhwydd,
Mynych dwyll amwyll ymwrdd,
Fy nhalcen wrth ben y bwrdd,
Lle'r oedd cawg yrhawg yn rhydd
A llafar badell efydd.
Syrthio o'r bwrdd, dragwrdd drefn,
A'r ddeudrestl a'r holl ddodrefn.
Rhoi diasbad o'r badell,
I'm hôl y'i clywid ymhell.
Gweiddi, gŵr gorwag oeddwn,
O'r cawg, a chyfarth o'r cŵn.

     Haws codi, drygioni drud,
Yn drwsgl nog yn dra esgud.
Dyfod, bu chwedl edifar,
I fyny, Cymry a'm câr,
Lle'r oedd garllaw muroedd mawr
Drisais mewn gwely drewsawr
Yn trafferth am eu triphac,
Hicin a Siencin a Siac.
Syganai'r delff soeg enau,
Aruthr o ddig, wrth y ddau:

'Mae Cymro, taer gyffro twyll,
Yn rhodio yma'n rhydwyll;
Lleidr yw ef, os goddefwn,
'Mogelwch, cedwch rhag hwn.'

Codi o'r ostler niferoedd
I gyd, a chwedl dybryd oedd.
Gygus oeddynt i'm gogylch
Bob naw i'm ceisiaw o'm cylch,
A minnau, hagr wyniau hyll,
Yn tewi yn y tywyll.
Gweddïais, nid gwedd eofn,
Dan gêl, megis dyn ag ofn,
Ac o nerth gweddi gerth gu,
Ac o ras y gwir Iesu,
Cael i minnau, cwlm anun,
Heb sâl, fy henwal fy hun.
Dihengais i, da yng saint,
I Dduw'r archaf faddeuaint.

Svelte squire in tow
I came to a classy town.
With fine dining at fine expense.
I lodged in style at a cost,
At a noted hostelry,
Strutting my young stuff,
And, knocking back the wine,
I spotted a sexy girl
In the place, my heart's desire.
I set out my stall for her, sweetheart,
Slim, aglow with morning brightness.
So I bought roast – not just for show –
And fine wine for my darling …

With all asleep – apart from me
And my beauty – poor souls,
I skilfully made tracks
For her bed – cue disaster.
I came, and more's the pity,
A right real cropper.
I hit (paying the price)
My shin (poor leg!) upon
An offensive stool, courtesy
Of a careless ostler.
In situ, I struck – after this pell-mell
Jumping, and confounded confusion –
My forehead on a table's edge,
Upending jug and brassy
Blabber-mouth of a bowl.
That brought down the house,
Board, trestle, the whole bally lot,
Until echoes resounded lavishly
In my foundering wake.
In praise of my vanity, the jug gave a bawl,
While to finish things off dogs barked one and all.

Easier, sad to tell, to rise slowly,
Than hastily. But pluckily up
I rose, may my Welsh friends praise me,
Rousing sleepers from stinking beds,
Three men of England,
Hicking, Jenkins and Jack,
Each worried about his pedlar's pack.
One slobber-mouth said
To his stout comrades

'There's a Welshman lurking near,
Be prepared for his tricks
And sly wiles: he'll thieve
Given a chance, so
Watch him, take care.'

The ostler roused the whole house,
Such commotion and hullabaloo.
Avid for blood, they hunted me
High and low, while I carefully hid.
Ashamed of my tell-tale lusts,
Courting the dark,
I prayed, in cowering fear,
To merciful Christ,
And thus escaped, blessed
Be grace, to my own lair.
Thanked be the saints
For my fruitless adventure,
And to God my plea
For His infinite mercy.

Pursuing his pleasure, Dafydd ap Gwilym (*c*.1320–70) ends up causing a rumpus in the form of an encounter with three irate 'Saxon' lodgers. The setting of a tavern is significant, as such places were by Dafydd's time regularly visited by English traders and merchants, and thus lively centres both of commercial and of cultural exchange between Wales and England. They inadvertently instanced the frequent cultural interactions and the fluidity and hybridity of 'national' identities and loyalties in this new era.

Dafydd himself was a prime example. He was intimately dependent on the 'occupying' power, as several members of his family had held high office under the Crown, with one of them becoming Constable of the castle at Newcastle Emlyn. But Dafydd was a roving poet – he had taken to the road, as had all Welsh poets once they no longer had a prince's court as solid base. He was therefore reliant for food and shelter on the hospitality of traditional Welsh squire and yeoman families and the Cistercian monasteries across Wales that had surreptitiously 'gone native' and that had brought progressive agricultural practices, centred on

the grange, into the country. His sense of the doubleness of his identity and social situation is frequently expressed in his work through its playfulness, its compulsive punning, its dialogic structure, and its constant self-awareness. And in this poem it surfaces in the mockery, which is directed as much at himself as at the 'Saxons'.

Dafydd's remarkably daring innovations as a poet of genius working in the established manner of ancient bardic tradition similarly owed much to his instincts for cultural synthesis, as he experimentally combined inherited Welsh forms with cultural imports from continental Europe. Nor was he alone in his complex dualities. Survival for the Welsh following the death of Llywelyn and the terminal collapse of the old social and political order depended on nimbleness of cultural adaptation. The great poets of the period were simply the most prominent exemplars of this process of constant radical realignment. Although the rest of the population could not, of course, follow their example and take to the road, the ordinary people must

have had to improvise and readjust best they could to a new mobile order, in which incoming English requirements mixed confusingly with the remnants of native Welsh social arrangements.

There were undoubtedly those who thrived and prospered under such exhilaratingly volatile circumstances. But there were those – particularly such as had lost social influence and prestige – who sullenly toed the line but resented the penalties imposed upon the 'natives' and awaited their opportunity. And in Owain Glyndŵr (c.1354–1416) this army of the disaffected, much swollen by those who had suffered economically in the wake of the terrible Black Death, found their great liberating hero. Even more evidently than his near-contemporary, Dafydd, Glyndŵr was seemingly successfully integrated at a reasonably high level into the English society of the border regions, some of whose aristocratic leaders he had loyally served in a lowly, but not insignificant, capacity in continental wars. But then something happened to alienate him, and he quite suddenly reconnected himself to Welsh legendary history and presented himself rebelliously as the political messiah long prophesied by the poets.

His ambitions were progressive and visionary – a Welsh parliament, a Welsh university, a Welsh church, a strategic diplomatic alliance with France. The successes of the troublesome Welshman were startlingly spectacular but ultimately fruitless. Reinforced by rather fragile strategic alliances, Glyndŵr came within an ace of establishing a viable, independent Welsh polity. But eventually faced with a powerful force led by the king's son, the future arch warmonger (and patron saint of Englishness) Henry V, Glyndŵr was defeated. And then he disappeared from view, fuelling long-lasting Welsh dreams of his messianic return one day. He remains 'the Welshness in all Welsh people, whether they know it or not', as Jan Morris once crisply put it. With his final defeat and mysterious disappearance, any faint hope there might have been for the return of at least some degree of Welsh self-government finally expired. Although the Tudors and their fateful Act of Union still lay more than a century ahead, from now on it was already in reality a case of 'for Wales, see England'.

Along with a quarter of the population, the Black Death had swept away the remains of the feudal system, thus liberating the poor from serfdom and opening the way to the formation of a peasantry that slowly prospered. While the lords of the March increasingly lost interest in Welsh affairs, new native classes of squires of varying wealth and power emerged along with an incipient minor bourgeoisie that began to occupy the small towns and thriving ports. A woollen industry developed, and drovers opened trails to London markets. Meanwhile, consciousness of nationhood was conserved by a brilliant constellation of strict metre poets.

The World

seventeenth century

I saw Eternity the other night
Like a great Ring of pure and endless light,
    All calm, as it was bright,
And round beneath it, time in hours, days, years
    Driv'n by the spheres
Like a vast shadow mov'd, in which the world
    And all her train were hurld;
The doting lover in his queintest strain
    Did there complain,
Near him, his lute, his fancy, and his flights,
    Wits sour delights
With gloves, and knots the silly snares of pleasure
    Yet his dear treasure
All scatter'd lay, while he his eys did pour
    Upon a flowr.

The darksome states-man hung with weights and woe
Like a thick midnight fog mov'd there so slow
    He did not stay, nor go;
Condemning thoughts (like sad eclipses) scowl
    Upon his soul,
And clouds of crying witnesses without
    Pursued him with one shout.
Yet dig'd the mole, and lest his ways be found
    Workt under ground,
Where he did clutch his prey, but one did see
    That policie,
Churches and altars fed him, perjuries
    Were gnats and flies,
It rain'd about him blood and tears, but he
    Drank them as free.

The fearfull miser on a heap of rust
Sate pining all his life there, did scarce trust
    His own hands with the dust,
Yet would not place one peece above, but lives
    In feare of theeves.
Thousands there were as frantick as himself
    And hug'd each one his pelf,
The down-right epicure plac'd heav'n in sense
    And scorned pretence
While others slipt into a wide excess
    Said little lesse;
The weaker sort slight, triviall wares inslave
    Who think them brave,
And poor, despised truth sate counting by
    Their victory.

Yet some, who all this while did weep and sing,
And sing, and weep, soar'd up into the Ring,
    But most would use no wing.
O fools (said I) thus to prefer dark night
    Before true light,
To live in grots, and caves, and hate the day
    Because it shews the way,
The way which from this dead and dark abode
    Leads up to God,
A way where you might tread the sun, and be
    More bright than he.
But as I did their madnes so discusse
    One whisper'd thus,
This Ring the Bride-groom did for none provide
    But for his bride.

'Wales ... is incorporated, annexed, united and subject to and under the imperial Crown of this realm.' The 1536 Act of Union minced no words and made no bones about it: 'Union' in this case meant annexation and incorporation. No longer allowed even a modicum of separate satellite existence, Wales was swallowed up by England. Or that was the plan. And in some ways it only confirmed what had already been steadily happening since 1282. Moreover, Wales indisputably benefited from this uncompromising arrangement which banished the Welsh language from the realms of law and government, created both the modern shire structure, and ensured Welsh representation in parliament.

The upwardly mobile Welsh squirearchy flourished in Tudor London as never before. Stubbornly Catholic though most of the population remained, their native language was immeasurably enriched and fitted for serious, even exalted, use by the 1588 translation into it of the Bible in its entirety, by the Anglican Bishop William Morgan and his learned patriotic associates – the earliest example by a long chalk of the Scriptures in other than one of the major languages of Europe. It was a period when the new-born Church of England made an invaluable long-term contribution to the preservation of a Welsh language and culture. But (exiled) Catholic, as well as Protestant, scholars served their country well. The first Welsh Grammarian to absorb the New Learning, Gruffydd Robert, was a major figure under Cardinal Borremeo in the Counter-Reformation movement in Milan, and introduced Renaissance humanism to Welsh attention. Other distinguished lexicographers and Grammarians included William Salesbury, Siôn Dafydd Rhys and John Davies of Mallwyd, while Humphrey Llwyd began to examine traditional Welsh legendary historiography. The work of this remarkable generation of Renaissance Humanists helped ensure that Welsh became a modern language, paving the way for a sophisticated literacy and preparing the ground for the astonishing scientific and philological discoveries of the prodigious polymath Edward Lhuyd at the end of the seventeenth century.

But the country was never remotely wealthy enough to support the bourgeois and urban culture that flourished in England from the Elizabeth period onwards. Overwhelmingly rural and backward, Wales sank into a quietist somnolence, disturbed only by the rude incursion, from across the border, of the Civil War disturbances that rocked and revolutionised England. The progressive forces of Puritans and Parliamentarians were very thin on the ground in poor, conservative Wales where the bulk of the population remained Anglo-Catholic in loyalties, although the anglicised gentry class was much more divided and polarised. But well before the conflict, Puritanism had begun to find pockets of support along the borders. During the Commonwealth, indeed, there were sufficient native Puritans available to implement the special bill enacted by Parliament with the intention of enlightening the benighted Welsh population by purifying the corrupt Anglican church in Wales.

Outraged by such measures, Henry Vaughan (1621–95), a staunch if maverick Anglican and an Oxford-educated minor gentleman of the Usk valley, turned to composing visionary poems. In their decidedly idiosyncratic and unorthodox way, these supplied the rituals, sacraments and teachings of which his self-imposed exile from his church had deprived him. Published under the title of *Silex Scintillans*, his two-part collection (completed in 1655) became one of the great classics of 'English' literature and an important example of Welsh writing in English. There was a cultural irony in that Vaughan was a lowly, minor offshoot of a powerful family that had once been renowned for sustaining Welsh bardic culture but that had, like most others of the same class, become steadily more anglicised. Yet, for all his English classical training at Oxford, the Welsh-speaking Vaughan retained a contact with the native culture that his privileged education had been designed to separate him from.

Three hundred years after Dafydd ap Gwilym, Vaughan thus still instanced, albeit in a poetry now written in English, that internal dividedness that had become the secret brand of the Welsh ever since the death of Llywelyn. This can be seen even in such a poem from *Silex Scintillans* as 'The World'. Ostensibly an orthodox poem of Christian expectation of millennial spiritual deliverance, it secretly expresses the age-old Welsh politico-cultural fantasy of apocalyptic messianic restoration of lost power. Given this longstanding expectation ingrained in native Welsh culture it wasn't surprising, after all, that not only did it find expression in Vaughan's Anglican poem but also that, long after the 'mainstream' Puritan sects in England had abandoned all hope of a miraculous Second Coming of Christ, a small though influential segment of Welsh Puritans of the revolutionary English group known as the 'Fifth Monarchists' stubbornly continued to believe in it.

No wonder Vaughan was fixated on eternity. Poverty, want, disease and early death wandered the countryside freely, particularly prone to visit the hovels of the poor labourers and husbandmen, who found refuge in a fertile culture of superstition. Above them were stacked the other classes – the rural craftsmen, merchants, professional classes, and so on up to the yeomen and the squirearchy. There were however precious few real toffs in a notoriously unruly country dependent on a scrapeacre subsistence economy and newly 'pacified' by English law, as administered by English magistrates, sheriffs and judges, that (unlike previous Welsh law) required married women to relinquish all property to their husbands. As for the squires, many of them grew plumply prosperous by such unscrupulous means as Vaughan had tabulated – landgrabs, aggressive litigation, advantageous marriages, sly social advancements and the like. In the end, power in Wales became concentrated in the hands of a mere two dozen prominent families, an arrangement that lasted down to the beginning of the twentieth century.

As Puritanism gradually evolved into Dissent, and the fledgling denominations slowly established a foothold in a religiously conservative Wales, so some experienced harassment from the agencies of Church and State. Quakers were driven in 1686 from the Dolgellau area to resettle under the patronage of William Penn in the 'Welsh Tract' in Pennsylvania, where two centuries later the renowned women's Liberal College of Bryn Mawr – named after the Dolgellau estate of a prominent emigrant Welsh Quaker – was established on the appropriately named Meirion Avenue. Yale, another seventeenth-century foundation named for Elihu Yale, from a leading family in Iâl, near Wrexham.

Meanwhile, in 1603, a 'Great Britain' was born from the union of the crowns of England and Scotland. Hereafter the Welsh could happily boast of being 'British', with the added kudos of believing (as no-one else did!) that they, after all, had been the *original* Britons back in the very earliest Christian centuries.

ANON.

Hen Benillion
Harp stanzas
eighteenth century

Dwedwch, fawrion o wybodaeth,
O ba beth y gwnaethpwyd hiraeth,
A pha ddeunydd a roed ynddo,
Na ddarfyddai wrth ei wisgo?

Derfydd aur, a derfydd arian,
Derfydd melfed, derfydd sidan,
Derfydd pob dilledyn helaeth,
Ond, er hyn, ni dderfydd hiraeth.

Hiraeth mawr a hiraeth creulon
Sy bob dydd yn torri 'nghalon,
Pan fwy dryma'r nos yn cysgu
Fe ddaw hiraeth, ac a'm deffry.

Hiraeth, hiraeth, cilia, cilia,
Paid â phwyso mor drwm arnaf,
Nesa dipyn at yr erchwyn,
Gad i mi gael cysgu gronyn.

Tell me, scholars of great learning
What makes the warp and weft of longing?
What material's woven in it,
That lasts however much one wears it?

Gold and silver soon wear out,
Silk and velvet need a clout;
All materials have an ending.
This is never true of longing.

Great and cruel is all longing –
Because of it my heart is breaking
When I lie in bed asleep
Longing wakes me up to weep.

Longing, longing, leave me, leave me
Do not press so heavy on me.
Move over in the bed, I weep,
Let me have a little sleep.

The lives of the ordinary masses of past centuries remain forever obstinately closed to us, in Wales as everywhere else. Yet their labours and experiences were the real stuff of which 'history' was made. For them, relatively little changed right down to the nineteenth century. Wales was still an overwhelmingly rural country, for all the bustle of its coastal towns and villages, where many of the menfolk went to sea as far as the Newfoundland fisheries, and of inland production centres like Newtown, where flannel and textile industries flourished on a small scale – a milieu that helped inform the visionary pioneering socialism of Robert Owen (who became another Welsh export to the USA).

Yet the richest parts of the countryside were barred to the rural population, having long been appropriated by the class of anglicised, and usually absent, gentry, both minor and major, that had flourished ever since Tudor times. The Enclosure Acts that began in the later eighteenth century aggravated this arrangement by legitimising landgrabs on a substantial scale, reducing many of the already struggling 'peasantry' to a state of poverty. That, in due course, helped encourage waves of mass migrations to the 'goldfields' of the astonishing new iron works of the Merthyr-Dowlais area that were soon to supply the growing railway systems of the world. But enclosures were also part of the revolution in agrarian production that made possible the feeding of the growing populations of urban centres and industrial districts.

The population at large was totally illiterate, until circulating schools teaching young pupils to read the Bible were introduced in 1731 at the church in Llanddowror by the enlightened vicar Griffith Jones, an initiative significantly strengthened and extended in due course by the Methodists. It resulted in around half the population of Wales becoming literate, and it attracted the attention of Catherine the Great of Russia. As recently as 1955, it was commended by UNESCO as a model for developing countries worldwide. The only path to 'advanced' learning was another native initiative, in the form of the 'Academies' for training ministers established by sects such as the Congregationalists and Baptists – institutions infinitely superior to the Oxford and Cambridge colleges (for Anglicans only), since they disregarded classical learning in favour of the independent-minded rational enquiry that powered the new natural sciences, economic sciences and political sciences of the day.

The most famous product of these Academies was Richard Price, whose thinking profoundly influenced that of the founders of the United States of America, and who was so admired by the French Revolutionaries that he was invited to join their Assembly. In moving out of Wales and settling in London, Price was emulating the movement of that small group, the London Welsh *intelligentsia* of antiquarians, philologists, grammarians, literary scholars and the like. It was these who, without benefit of university, began the work of piecing laboriously together the history of their people and their culture from their very beginnings in the mists of the 'dark ages', thus laying the foundations for a new Welsh nationhood a century later.

These intellectuals were, of course, thoroughly bilingual, whereas the ordinary people were almost without exception monoglot speakers of Welsh, even though most of the key positions in their society – in law, trade, church, political life and so on – were occupied by monoglot English-speakers. And since Welsh Wales had no affluent urban centres that could support a professional entertainment culture, it had to make do with home-grown events and talents. So whereas an anglicised town like Swansea, already home to an important copper industry, could attract theatrical touring companies from England, the rest of Wales depended on the inventiveness of a local genius like Twm o'r Nant, whose home-spun plays provided a lively running commentary on the life of the times. And to enliven the long winter evenings, 'nosweithiau llawen' were organised – boisterous, and no doubt frequently coarse, programmes of improvised entertainments. It was on occasions such as these that folk songs and verses would be sung to harp accompaniment – just as ballads were immensely popular features of rural fairs (and indeed, in due course, industrial gatherings) right across Wales, and functioned as the 'newspapers' of the people.

Wele'n sefyll rhwng y myrtwydd
See – there stands
early nineteenth century

Wele'n sefyll rhwng y myrtwydd
    Wrthrych teilwng o fy mryd,
Er mai o ran, yr wy'n adnabod
    Ei fod uchlaw gwrthrychau'r byd:
        Henffych fore
    Y caf ei weled fel y mae.

Rhosyn Saron yw ei enw,
    Gwyn a gwridog, teg o bryd;
Ar ddeng mil y mae'n rhagori
    O wrthrychau penna'r byd:
        Ffrind pechadur,
    Dyma ei beilot ar y môr.

Beth sydd imi mwy a wnelwyf
    Ag eilunod gwael y llawr?
Tystio'r wyf nad yw eu cwmni
    I'w cystadlu â Iesu mawr:
        O! am aros
    Yn ei gariad ddyddiau f'oes.

See – there stands – among the myrtles –
An object worthy of my heart –
Though I only know in part how
He transcends all worldly thought –
Welcome – morning –
When I see him – as he is –

He is named the Rose of Sharon –
White and ruddied – fair of face –
He surpasses the ten thousand
Foremost – things – the world contains –
Friend – of sinners –
He – their pilot through the sea –

Why should I deal – any longer –
With base – idols – of the earth –
Their whole company – I swear it –
Is no match – for Jesus' worth –
Oh – to linger –
All my days – within his love –

Wales did, however, undergo one profound transformative change during the eighteenth century. A reforming movement within the Anglican Church, called 'the Methodists' because of the system of meetings they arranged to support and strengthen faith, derided as 'Enthusiasts' and dismissed as 'Jumpers', began to appeal to ordinary people and to grow with spectacular speed. As its remarkable network of institutions spread across the whole country, so this reforming Anglican sect began to develop into a distinctly separate, and distinctively Welsh, independent denomination. Inspired by evangelical preachers and writers of genius, such as William Williams of Pantycelyn ('Guide me oh thou great Jehovah'), Methodism became the ordinary people's religion of choice, and the ecstatic hymns it produced in seeming abundance became their gospel songs of faith.

Unable to contain her spiritual passion, Ann Griffiths (1776–1805), a farm girl from mid-Wales of little formal education, began to compose impromptu hymns of praise that have survived thanks only to their being committed to memory by her maid and thus handed down to posterity.

The translation included here is one by the American Joseph P. Clancy that imitates the unconventional punctuation of the great nineteenth-century American poet Emily Dickinson, in an attempt to convey the impromptu ejaculations of Griffiths's ecstatic style.

Since they were still deeply conservative in their social and political sympathies, the loyalist Welsh people were generally antipathetic to the radicalism unleashed by the French Revolution and promoted by that charlatan of genius Iolo Morganwg. But early in the nineteenth century, the national outlook began to change as Methodism entered into an informal alliance with the already established denominational churches of the Baptists and Congregationalists/Independents. This 'Nonconformist' alliance became the powerhouse of dynamic social and political change that turned Wales into an increasingly literate and increasingly militant society.

As the Welsh began to incubate a new identity as a 'Nonconformist nation', so a rapidly industrialising country became known beyond its borders for its 'dangerous' insurrectionary radicalism. This was expressed alike through the rural protests against toll-gates known as 'the Rebecca Riots' (early 1840s), the march on Newport (1839) by a demonstration in favour of an enlightened political Charter (the Chartists), and the profound unrest and disquiet in the very cradle of modern industrial society (at Dowlais-Merthyr) that led to a 'proletarian' uprising branded 'the Merthyr Riots' (1831) and produced the first people's martyr in Dic Penderyn.

Nonconformist Wales was further outraged into radical protest by the findings of Government inspectors from England in 1847 that its religion was benighted, its language primitive and backward, its women given to immorality, and its educated intelligence minimal. For half a century and more following this mid-century report, chapel society, simmering with anger, devoted itself to demonstrating its impeccable respectability by strictly limiting and policing the role of women, anxiously cultivating musical talents, and generally trumpeting its Victorian virtues, while it also set about producing an extraordinary generation of social activists and political giants, all belonging to the progressive wing of the British Liberal Party. Between them, these politicians worked to lessen the influence of the 'foreign' Church of England and to reform the abuses that enraged the farming community. They also established a widespread system of state-funded schools, a new national university, a national library and national museum, and several other key institutions of modern nationhood. It was burgeoning national pride that was captured in 'Hen Wlad Fy Nhadau', the song composed in Pontypridd in 1858 that went on to be adopted as Wales's national anthem. And that same pride led to the adoption of the Red Dragon as the country's national flag – the emblem dates back to the wyvern that fluttered on the flags of the Roman legionaries.

It has been open season on Welsh chapels for a long time now. The privilege of hindsight has been enthusiastically abused, and they have been endlessly lectured on their sins (sexism, rabid anti-Catholicism etc.). Their intolerance of theological differences resulted in the persecution of the small community of Unitarians, driving families such as the Lloyds of Cardiganshire to emigrate to the US, where a proud descendant, Frank Lloyd Wright, became the most distinguished American architect of the twentieth century. Yes, the chapels had their obvious faults, but they have come to be treated as the institutional equivalent of Rasputin, sinister institutions capable of returning from the seeming dead, and so needing to be repeatedly subdued by frenzied attack. Yet, once the hysteria of self-righteousness is allowed to subside, what still shines steadily through is their fundamental decency and valuable service to Wales.

Nonconformist Wales, its heartland being the rural west and north, was a remarkable religious, cultural and political phenomenon. For all its regrettable repressive tendencies, hypocrisies and iniquities, it enabled the transformation of an ancient people into a modern, complex and increasingly literate nation. Its innumerable chapels, 'squat as toads', were not only dynamic religious institutions, they were grass-roots initiatives, supplying ordinary people with educational opportunities, social orientation, political training, and eventually a range of leisure and cultural activities. These self-help bodies saw off the powerful state Church of England. It had once rendered glorious service to Welsh culture, but by the nineteenth century had become little better than a foreign succubus, feeding greedily off the Welsh people. Rural Wales was at long last liberated from the tyranny of tenantry as predatory landlords were called to account; a new, experimental, industrial 'civilization' was slowly regulated; and, for the first time, a Welsh middle-class enabled to evolve – although sadly at the expense of alienating the growing mass of a working population increasingly reliant on a remarkable emergent generation of secular labour leaders of its own production. Several of Nonconformity's nineteenth-century leaders earned a deserved reputation for enlightened opposition to several forms of oppression, including slavery.

Mercifully, Wales had long been protected by its poverty from exploitative involvement in the slave trade. Yet some individuals had benefited from it, both at home and abroad. Some of the early seventeenth-century settlers in the US Southern States had become plantation owners – hence the prominence of Welsh surnames among black Americans, from such famous athletes as Florence Griffith Joyner (Flo-Jo) to statesmen of the calibre of Colin Powell. Almost a tenth of the surnames of today's residents of South Carolina are of Welsh origin. Jefferson Davis, President of the Confederate States, was of Welsh descent, as were figures associated with John Wilkes Booth in the assassination of Lincoln (who was himself of Ysbyty Ifan and Bala descent, and had 100,000 Welsh-language pamphlets printed for his 1860 presidential election). By contrast, the Welsh of Ohio fought valiantly in Union ranks.

The colourful 'pirate' Henry Morgan of Captain Morgan rum fame ended up owning 'Llanrumney planation' in

Jamaica, effectively a slave labour camp; Sir Thomas Picton, hero of Waterloo, had an appalling record of mistreatment of black people as vicious military commander in Trinidad; the Pennant family of Disneyesque Penrhyn Castle made their second fortune out of North Wales quarrying – their first had come from plantations in Jamaica. Across the Caribbean, black people were routinely electrocuted, maimed, beaten to a pulp, decapitated, drawn and quartered, roasted alive over a slow fire, or publicly starved to death. And in its heyday, Swansea, the world's Copperopolis and a centre of Welsh abolitionism, imported its ore from Cuba, where black and Chinese labour were worked to death in the mines. The modern reputation of the prominent Victorian explorer Henry Morton Stanley – born John Rowlands, and forever remembered for his supposed 'Doctor Livingstone, I presume?' greeting – has been irretrievably damaged by his dubious involvement in the notorious 'experiments' of King Leopold II of Belgium in the African Congo.

The export version of Welsh Nonconformity also had a chequered record. Missionaries exhibited cultural condescension while demonstrating heroic courage. The hospital at Wuhan, China, which was the epicentre of the coronavirus epidemic, was established by the remarkable Gruffydd John of Swansea. The Khasia hills of Northern India still echo to the sound of Welsh hymn-tunes imported by Welsh missionaries. David Jones and David Griffiths left their mark in Madagascar, establishing the orthography of Malagasy and translating the Bible into that language.

Lloyd George, the greatest political product of this Nonconformist background and the only Welshman to become Prime Minister of a Britain then still in the full flush of its world-wide power – another Welsh-speaking Welshman, Billy Hughes, was at the very same time Prime Minister of Australia, and Charles Evans Hughes was the Republican candidate for the Presidency of the USA – illustrated in his own duality the two most prominent strands of Welsh life at the turn of the century. One strand tied Wales proudly into the British Empire that Wales had helped establish – hadn't Merthyr cannon roared for Wellington at Waterloo? Welsh troops had been involved in the Afghan campaigns, were prominent in the Zulu wars, present at Mafeking, and helped loot Beijing's Summer Palace. Lord Tredegar (who numbered slave-owners among his ancestors) was one of only two survivors of the Charge of the Light Brigade. And by the late nineteenth century, Wales underpinned the Empire with its new-found industrial might. The other strand – dating back to the pioneering work of the London Welsh intelligentsia at the end of the eighteenth century – was highly patriotic, as proud of the cultural richness of the ancient Welsh past as it was of the remarkable achievements of the new industrial Wales, and it sought recognition by Britain of its prominent status as a regional nation in the form of a limited degree of self-government.

But by the outbreak of the First World War, Liberal and Nonconformist Wales was already on the wane, and thereafter never really recovered. Its last hurrah was the remarkable religious Revival of 1904–5 led by the charismatic Evan Roberts, the Ivor Novello of Welsh evangelists, whose ripple effects reached as far as the US and India. In retrospect, it seems increasingly like the death-dance of a great religious culture – rather like the Buffalo Dance of the doomed Sioux before the end of their world at Wounded Knee.

Nonconformity's demise was in part due to the greater strength of the newer Wales that had been steadily forming in the newly industrialised valleys of the South Wales coalfield during the latter decades of the nineteenth century, a development that rocketed Wales in a few short decades from provincial obscurity to what Karl Marx might have termed 'world historical' significance. In 1850, just over a million people lived in Wales: by 1914, the total was two and a half million, two thirds of whom lived in the industrialised south-east of the country. By the 1900s, the English language, the *lingua franca* of this astonishing new cosmopolitan society, had displaced the Welsh language. Nevertheless, the next half-century saw a remarkable revival of Welsh-language writing, which was accompanied by the emergence of a generation of highly talented English-language writers, which included Dylan Thomas.

As for the huge working population employed not only in the iron and steel industries but also in the deep mines, whose winding machinery had erupted like a black rash across the landscape, it began to consolidate by painful degrees into a new kind of self-protective collective, the 'working class'. This meant the majority of the Welsh

were no longer a Nonconformist people, but a raw
and increasingly militant industrial proletariat, which
eventually looked to a new political party of its own
birthing, the Labour Party, for leadership. Before long,
even Lloyd George – the architect of the Welfare State
before the First World War (thanks to the Old Age Pension
scheme he introduced as Chancellor in 1908), the man
who destroyed the power of the landed aristocrats (the
'People's Budget' of 1909), and the instigator of National
Insurance (1911) – was to be replaced by Aneurin Bevan
as the people's darling, and it was Bevan who was credited
with the foundation of the National Health Service in the
aftermath of the Second World War.

It was unfortunate, however, that so many of the
leaders of Welsh Socialism were to espouse what has been
termed 'a naive cosmopolitanism', thereby contributing
substantially to the anglicisation of the country. Equally
unfortunate was the great reluctance of traditional Wales,
rural, chapel-going, Welsh-speaking and ardently Liberal,
to acknowledge the new, 'foreign' brand of Welshness
being produced in 'the Valleys' – an attitude reflected
in the exclusionary cultural politics of Cymru Fydd, a
movement that otherwise furnished late Victorian and
Edwardian Wales with several noble national institutions.
The rift was to hamper the development of a modern,
inclusive, consciousness of being Welsh for most of the
twentieth century. One sadly absurd consequence was
that, in the context of Wales, 'national' and 'international'
came for long to be treated as mutually exclusive terms.

The Great War was a watershed event in Wales as across Europe. Initially reluctant to get involved, the Nonconformists and the proletariat alike eventually rallied to Lloyd George's impassioned pleas, with the exception of a few principled leaders of the chapels and the miners. Carnage on the Somme duly ensued, most particularly at Ypres. But women, at least and at last, benefited from the war effort, gaining the vote for all over the age of thirty at war's end, having proved efficient at taking over many of the occupations traditionally reserved for men. And the modern Welfare State was a by-product of such radical wartime innovations by Lloyd George as the nationalisation of mines, of shipping and of railways.

Even home rule seemed briefly within reach, in the wake of US President Woodrow Wilson's support for the self-determination of small peoples. After all, hadn't Lloyd George's wartime appeal for Welsh support been based on inflating their egos by trumpeting their prowess as one of the world's little 'five-foot-five' nations? As for the education system, arrogantly anglophone right up to university level (Progress = English), that had been established by the end of the nineteenth century, while it nurtured a stellar generation of talent in both Welsh and English (and in due course littered England with teachers), it also probably did more harm to the long-term future of the Welsh language than any other single development. And it tied Wales firmly (and probably irrevocably) into modern British society, but exclusively on England's terms.

The failure of mainstream British politics to address

Wales's distinctive needs after 1918 led to the formation of Plaid Cymru in 1925, the national party of Wales, that first impacted strongly on public attention in 1936, when three of its leading figures set fire to a government training school for aerial bombers established, in the teeth of Wales-wide opposition, in the heart of the Llŷn peninsula, an ancient stronghold of Welsh culture.

Y Meirwon
The Dead
twentieth century

Bydd dyn wedi troi'r hanner cant yn gweld yn lled glir
   Y bobl a'r cynefin a foldiodd ei fywyd e',
A'r rhaffau dur a'm deil dynnaf wrthynt hwy
   Yw y beddau mewn dwy fynwent yn un o bentrefi'r De.

Wrth yrru ar feisiglau wedi eu lladrata o'r sgrap
   A chwarae rygbi dros Gymru â phledrenni moch,
Ni freuddwydiais y cawn glywed am ddau o'r cyfoedion hyn
   Yn chwydu eu hysgyfaint i fwced yn fudr goch.

Ein cymdogion, teulu o Ferthyr Tudful oeddent hwy,
   'Y Merthyron' oedd yr enw arnynt gennym ni,
Saethai peswch pump ohonynt, yn eu tro, dros berth yr ardd
   I dorri ar ein hysgwrs ac i dywyllu ein sbri.

Sleifiem i'r parlyrau beiblaidd i sbïo yn syn
   Ar olosg o gnawd yn yr arch, ac ar ludw o lais;
Yno y dysgasom uwch cloriau wedi eu sgriwio cyn eu pryd
   Golectau gwrthryfel coch a litanïau trais.

Nid yr angau a gerdd yn naturiol fel ceidwad cell
   Â rhybudd yn sŵn cloncian ei allweddi llaith,
Ond y llewpart diwydiannol a naid yn sydyn slei,
   O ganol dŵr a thân, ar wŷr wrth eu gwaith.

Yr angau hwteraidd: yr angau llychlyd, myglyd, meddw,
    Yr angau a chanddo arswyd tynghedfen las;
Trôi tanchwa a llif-pwll ni yn anwariaid, dro,
    Yn ymladd â phwerau catastroffig, cyntefig, cas.

Gwragedd dewrfud â llond dwrn o arian y gwaed,
    A bwcedaid o angau yn atgo tan ddiwedd oes,
Yn cario glo, torri coed-tân a dodi'r ardd
    yn darllen yn amlach hanes dioddefaint y groes.

Gosodwn Ddydd Sul y Blodau ar eu beddau bwys
    O rosynnau silicotig a lili mor welw â'r nwy,
A chasglu rhwng y cerrig annhymig a rhwng yr
                                            anaeddfed gwrb
    Yr hen regfeydd a'r cableddau yn eu hangladdau hwy.

Diflannodd yr Wtopia oddi ar gopa Gellionnen,
    Y ddynoliaeth haniaethol, y byd diddosbarth a di-ffin;
Ac nid oes a erys heddiw ar waelod y cof
    Ond teulu a chymdogaeth, aberth a dioddefaint dyn.

With his fiftieth birthday behind him, a man sees with fair clarity
  The people and surroundings that made him what he is,
And the steel ropes that tether me strongest to these things
  In a village of the South, are the graves in two cemeteries.

I'd ride a bike pilfered from scrap, or with a pig's bladder
  Play rugby for Wales; and all that while,
Little thought I'd hear how two of my contemporaries
  Would spew into a bucket their lungs red and vile.

Our neighbours they were, a family from Merthyr Tydfil,
  The 'martyrs' we called them, by way of a pun,
And five of them by turns had a cough that crossed the fences
  To break up our chatter and darken all our fun.

We crept in the Bibled parlours, and peeped with awe
  At cinders of flesh in the coffin, and ashes of song,
And there we learnt, over lids screwed down before their time,
  Collects of red revolt and litanies of wrong.

Not the death that goes his natural rounds, like a gaol warder,
  Giving notice in the clink of his damp keys,
But the leopard of industry leaping sudden and sly
  That strikes from fire and water men to their knees.

The hootering death: the dusty, smokeful, drunken death,
   Death whose dreadful grey destiny was ours;
Explosion and flood changed us often into savages
   Fighting catastrophic and devilish powers.

Mute and brave women with a fistful of bloodmoney,
   With a bucketful of death, forever the rankling of loss,
Carrying coal, chopping wood for a fire, or setting the garden,
   And more and more reading the Passion of the Cross.

This Sunday of Flowers, as we place on their graves a bunch
   Of silicotic roses and lilies pale as gas,
Between the premature stone and the curb yet unripened,
   We gather the old blasphemings, curses of funerals past.

Our Utopia vanished from the top of Gellionnen,
   Our abstract humanity's classless, defrontiered reign,
And today nothing is left at the deep root of the mind
   Save family and neighbourhood, man's sacrifice and pain.

A native of the heavily industrialised Swansea Valley, D. Gwenallt Jones had seen his father die when a crucible of white-hot metal spilled on his unprotected head. It seared a Bosch-like vision in his memory of the hellish, barbaric character of industrialism as experienced by its victims, the huge workforce needed to feed the cannibalistic monster. Silhouetted defiantly against that dark back-cloth were the fierce solidarities of proletarian life, the utopian dreams of an exploited population's international socialism, the consoling beliefs nurtured in those great, gaunt, forbidding sanctuaries of the people, the chapels. Already a fiercely committed member of the Independent Labour Party at the age of eighteen, Gwenallt had refused to serve in the capitalists' war in 1914, and been grimly imprisoned in Dartmoor.

Having experienced industrialism at its most horrific (the locust years of the Great Depression; the litany of terrible pit disasters culminating in Aberfan in 1966, when 144 people, mostly primary school children, were killed by the slip of coal slurry), and, at its most epic (the honourable socialist dreams of a more just society for everyone everywhere; the great strikes of the North Wales quarrymen, where almost 3,000 men stayed out at the Penrhyn quarry for a punishing three years; the stubborn, stoic defiance of the South Wales miners), and having relished its cultural products at their most heady (the intoxicating feats of Welsh rugby wizardry, the world-beating heroics of Valleys boxers, the glamour of film-stars like Stanley Baker and Richard Burton, the resonant diapasons of male voice choirs), Wales continues, even today to pride itself, with good reason, on having been one of the cradles of industrial civilisation.

Although there had been pockets of industrial activity across Wales before the late eighteenth century, from Parys Mountain on Anglesey and the North Wales quarries to the pottery works of the Swansea and Cardiff areas, dramatic change was first signalled by the rash of early fledgling industrial ventures of the north-east, and the growth of Swansea into Wales's largest town thanks to the development of a major copper industry. But dramatic transformation came only with the development in the Merthyr-Dowlais area of a string of major iron works totalling eighteen in number by 1815. The workers benefited from better income than in the rural areas, but lived in the filth and squalor of circumstances that readily bred typhus, typhoid, tuberculosis and a terrible cholera epidemic in 1849 – they also gradually bred new collectives, new solidarities, and a new, radical politics of protest, demonstration, even uprising.

By 1850, the population of Wales had doubled, and

only a third of a previously agrarian nation still worked on the land, the majority of them tenant farmers at the mercy of large estates. Originally merely the local source of coal for the iron works, deep mines began from the middle of the nineteenth century to supply England's urban centres with domestic coal, and eventually to export their highly desirable product all over the world in ships that were themselves powered by coal. Proliferating explosively in number as new mines were opened in the two great Rhondda valleys, they turned the South Wales coalfield into an industrial centre of global reach and importance, in the process sucking in a huge workforce of diverse background. In the Snowdonia region of the north-west, the quarries grew exponentially into some of the biggest to meet the demand for the slate that eventually 'roofed the world'. By the late nineteenth century, 80 per cent of British slate came from Caernarfonshire, and the Oakeley quarry was the largest in the world. A slump by century's end led to the great Penrhyn strike, a bitter, gruelling labour struggle that lasted three long years.

Meanwhile, South Wales, it has been said, had become the Persian Gulf of the period almost overnight, capable of turning the world's most precious power supply – coal, both anthracite and steam – on and off at will. The glamour and romance of its world dominance can be sensed even in the bare statistics: while 60 per cent of world coal exports left British ports, 40 per cent of that total sailed out of Welsh harbours – primarily from Newport and from the world's busiest coaling port, Cardiff. Industry and trains in France, Spain, Italy, Egypt, Brazil, Argentina, they all depended on Welsh coal.

At the heart of the region of the South Wales coalfield that produced the highly prized steam coal lay the two fabled Rhondda valleys, memorably described by the writer Gwyn Thomas as among 'Britain's darker marvels'. They were, he said, his Americanism deliberately gesturing towards this area's later affinities with the industrialising US, 'two deep gulches in the North Glamorgan hills', where 'pit shafts opened like the holes in a mature cheese'. And, he sadly added, 'never was a small stretch of earth so majestically ransacked'. That small stretch of earth also saw much heartbreak before story's end: it seems appropriate that the surname of the entrepreneur who sank the first viable pit in the Rhondda was Coffin.

By the end of the nineteenth century, there must have been more smoke being generated all over the globe by one black Welsh fossil fuel than all the fires of hell could match – and the very Devil himself must have been tempted to become a customer. It was perhaps in retaliation that he made those bold incursions into this territory, the deep mines of the Valleys, such infernally dangerous places in which to work. Of the 2,328 men killed underground in Britain during the last two decades of the nineteenth century, almost half were from Wales. Then in 1913 came the ultimate catastrophe, when 439 men lost their lives in Senghenydd: a whole community obliterated. And as for the miners 'lucky' enough to last the course, a grim percentage was left gasping for breath by 'the dust' – such a harmless domestic epithet for that cruel slow strangler, pneumoconiosis. Welsh coal was the world's blood jewel of its day, and Wales had become a one-industry nation – around half the population depended on the mining industry, a situation unequalled in Europe. This meant that when 'The Fed' (The South Wales Miners' Federation) was born in 1898, in the wake of a calamitous strike, Wales had a genuine national organisation of working men for the first time.

When in the 1920s the noted American writer H. L. Mencken visited Cardiff's docks area of Tiger Bay, noted for its Red Light district, he reckoned it included probably one of the largest concentrations of black people in the whole of Europe. As early as 1911, Butetown had contained a black community which, although small, was second in size only to that of London. Seamen from all over the world had settled there, as well as in the neighbouring docklands of Newport and Barry, and the area eventually became known for the intermarriage between immigrants and local girls. But in 1919, social conditions so heightened tensions between Yemenis, Somalians, Afro-Caribbeans and the surrounding white population, that ugly race rioting occurred. Other immigrant communities, such as those consisting of Jews or Irish or Italians, occasionally attracted similar hostility. Yet, by the Second World War, Tiger Bay – birthplace of Shirley Bassey, the incomparable Rugby League winger Billy Boston, and British heavyweight champion Joe Erskine, and sometime home to people of scores of different nationalities – had acquired a not altogether undeserved reputation for inter-racial harmony

As the coalfield began to suffer by the beginning of the twentieth century from competition from vast new industrial centres, such as those in the US (whose development had been ironically facilitated by skilled Welsh workers), so the unions the workers had formed turned increasingly militant and confrontational under a new, much more markedly socialist leadership, with some daring figures espousing syndicalism and worker ownership – a highpoint was the publication of the explosive work the *Miners' Next Step* in 1911. Of the confrontations that resulted, the most famous, fateful and violent occurred in Tonypandy in 1910, when Churchill – hissed forever after as the villain in Rhondda cinemas – sent in first the Metropolitan Police, and then the military to 'quell' what the capitalist press chose to misrepresent as a 'riot', turning Tonypandy into the 'Odessa and Sebastopol' of Britain. Equally violent was the confrontation in Llanelli in 1911, where railwaymen went on strike, and where again the military intervened, with tragic consequences.

By 1913, the coalfield employed a quarter of a million men and was responsible for a fifth of the coal production of Britain, with Cardiff – swollen by its wealth to substantial size and busily endowing itself with the civic dignity that became its scale and rank as one of the great cities of Empire – recognised as the greatest of the coal-exporting ports. The Third Marquis of Bute, who owned Cardiff docks, was the wealthiest man in the world. In

1904, the Coal Exchange saw the clinching of the first million pound deal. But from then on all was steady decline, as wages were slashed in half and labour relations turned increasingly sour and tense. By 1932, 42 per cent of miners were unemployed in South Wales, while in Bryn-mawr, at the epicentre of the crisis of the Welsh iron industry, upwards of 90 per cent had no jobs. Despite the miners' heroic (and sadly self-destructive) prolongation of the great General Strike of 1926, their work prospects became even more remote than their dreams of social and political justice.

Half a million people left the industrial wasteland of South Wales between the two wars, joining the thousands who had emigrated in the nineteenth century not only to the US (where skilled Welsh industrial workers provided the backbone of the new industrial society, particularly in states such as West Virginia, Ohio and Pennsylvania) and famously to Patagonia (where, in 1865, Welsh settlers had arrived to carve out a harsh new home far from the threat of encroaching Englishness), but also to London, the Midlands and, above all, to boom-time Liverpool. There, the numerous Welsh who thrived came by 1900 to constitute a grand 'high bourgeoisie' to which Wales itself could offer no parallel. By the mid-1930s, there were more than 5,000 Welsh people living in Slough, and by the census of 1951 it was estimated that almost 650,000 of the population of England had originated in Wales. For many, elsewhere had come to seem irresistibly enticing. No wonder that one little Valleys girl was moved to pray

in the 1930s to the Good Lord that 'Thy will be done in
Merthyr as well as in Devon'. An international socialism was
naturally appealing under such circumstances, and South
Wales mining communities, appalled by the treatment by
Franco of the brave miners of Asturias, sent more young
men to fight for the Republican cause in Spain than went
from any other region of Britain.

For those who remained in the blighted Valleys to face
the terrible 1930s, gross poverty led to malnourishment
and its associated afflictions. But although helplessness
stalked the Valleys, it was not accompanied by hopelessness.
The renowned social, religious and political solidarities of
the people held defiantly firm, and became embodied in
the figure of Tommy Farr from Tonypandy, whose thrilling
heavyweight fight with the great American world champion
Joe Louis at Madison Square Gardens immediately entered
the realms of legend. But long before Farr, previous heroes
of the ring, such as Freddie Welsh, Jim Driscoll, and the
incomparable little 'twt' from Tylorstown, Jimmy Wilde
(the 'ghost with a hammer in his hand', still regarded as
the greatest fly-weight of all time), had all triumphed in
the US and reigned as world champions. In that sadly
departed golden era, the Welsh rugby team had won the
Triple Crown no fewer than six times in twelve years, and
had beaten the invincible All Blacks of New Zealand in a
famously controversial game in 1906.

DYLAN THOMAS

Fern Hill

twentieth century

Now as I was young and easy under the apple boughs
About the lilting house and happy as the grass was green,
  The night above the dingle starry,
    Time let me hail and climb
  Golden in the heydays of his eyes,
And honoured among wagons I was prince of the apple towns
And once below a time I lordly had the trees and leaves
    Trail with daisies and barley
  Down the rivers of the windfall light.

And as I was green and carefree, famous among the barns
About the happy yard and singing as the farm was home,
  In the sun that is young once only,
    Time let me play and be
  Golden in the mercy of his means,
And green and golden I was huntsman and herdsman,
          the calves
Sang to my horn, the foxes on the hills barked clear and cold,
    And the sabbath rang slowly
  In the pebbles of the holy streams …

… Nothing I cared, in the lamb white days, that time
                                        would take me
Up to the swallow thronged loft by the shadow of my hand,
        In the moon that is always rising,
                Nor that riding to sleep
        I should hear him fly with the high fields
And wake to the farm forever fled from the childless land.
Oh as I was young and easy in the mercy of his means,
                Time held me green and dying
        Though I sang in my chains like the sea.

Dylan Thomas's 'Fern Hill' was his response to a world that had taken an appalling turn for the worst with the murderous explosions of the first ever nuclear bombs at Hiroshima and Nagasaki. His instinctive reaction was to return, in idyllic memory, to glorious golden days of childhood spent on holiday in his family's native region of rural West Wales. In the process he was actually reversing the journey his father, like hundreds of thousands of others of his kind and background, had undertaken from the impoverished rural west to the booming industrial east. In choosing to retrace his father's footsteps, it was as if Dylan Thomas were recognising that the boom times of industrial South Wales were well and truly over; as if in writing 'Fern Hill' he was writing an indirect elegy for a remarkable world of Wales that had disappeared for ever just as sadly and certainly as his own beloved home town of Swansea, one of Wales's most important industrial centres, had been obliterated by the Luftwaffe during the war. His (re)turn to refuge in the west was also reminiscent of the journey into the Welsh countryside taken by thousands of little children evacuated from England's great cities in order to escape the wartime bombing. Later, American GI's were also to penetrate to most corners of the country.

Post-war Wales remained the fiefdom of the British Labour Party it had been ever since the end of World War One. But Conservatism also increasingly began to offer valuable help to the language as well as a contribution to the creation of new institutions. As for Plaid Cymru, it continued to function as the nation's conscience. Having begun as a movement amongst Welsh-language writers and intellectuals, it slowly matured into a political party, winning its first seat at Westminster in 1966. This alarmed Welsh Labour sufficiently for it to organise, under the auspices of the oleaginous George Thomas, a grandiose (and highly controversial) ceremony of Investiture of the Prince of Wales in Caernarfon in 1969. The Investiture was the culmination of a troubled decade that included the major episode at Tryweryn (1962–3). There, the failure of the Welsh political establishment at Westminster to prevent a valley in mid-Wales rapidly becoming a 'Green Desert' from being drowned to supply Liverpool with water had brought home to a new generation the helpless, subaltern condition of Wales.

While the permanently precarious character of a separate Welsh identity was highlighted during the Second World War – at one time, there was government talk of moving four million women and children from English cities into the country – it survived the conflict with the key features of the post-industrial society of the post-war period already becoming clear as new trading estates primarily utilising female labour began to be established to replace the old heavy industries. But the strongly centralist approach dictated by wartime conditions continued to be a feature of the Attlee Labour government that established the Welfare State, while for Wales the most satisfying outcome of its nationalisation agenda was the creation of the National Coal Board in 1947.

Westminster investment was evident in the creation of economic development areas and the dramatic increase in employment in public services (particularly education and local government). In due course, Wales acquired bodies like the Vehicle Licensing Centre, the Passport Office, and the Royal Mint, which served the whole of Britain. The renowned Welsh steel and tinplate industries contracted dramatically along with the mining industry – although a huge new steel plant was created at Port Talbot and twinned with state-of-the-art tinplate works at Llanelli (Trostre) and Swansea (Felindre), while another mammoth steel plant was opened at Llanwern. Already by 1947, the number of miners working for what was now a nationalised industry was half what it had been in the 1920s, and by 1978 the workforce had dropped to a pitiful 36,000. And the cruel post-industrial process accelerated ruthlessly during the 1980s decade of the Thatcher governments, despite strong backing by South Wales miners powerfully supported by their wives for the ill-fated strike led by Arthur Scargill (1984–5).

Rural Wales, as hard-hit as the Depression Valleys during the 1930s, offered a similar sad picture of decline,

although a new prosperity did come through grants
and subsidies in the wake of the formation of a Milk
Marketing Board (an initiative of the 1930s). And from
the 1970s onwards, incomers, mostly from the south-east
of England, took advantage of falling house prices in the
Welsh countryside to buy holiday homes in desirable
areas, often with resultant catastrophic impact on the
local Welsh-speaking culture. Incomers totalled more
than 40,000 a year, while there were areas where they
accounted for more than 40 per cent of the population.

While extremists took to burning 'settler' cottages (cartoons sarcastically advertised 'Come Home to a Real Fire'), a generation of activists braved prison to secure a degree of parity – initially in the form of bilingual road signs – for the Welsh language for the first time in over four hundred years.

Partly and uncertainly offsetting this erosion of the culture was the dramatic increase in the number of young people in key urban areas such as Cardiff and Swansea who attended Welsh-medium primary and secondary schools. And the establishing – in the teeth of opposition – first of a radio channel in the language, and then a TV channel, helped ensure Welsh continued to be a vibrant contemporary medium. As a result, it is the world's only widely-spoken Celtic language. By steady degrees, too, Wales began at long last to acquire some of the political institutions of nationhood, with a bureaucracy to match, beginning with a Welsh Office with a strong Cardiff presence and answerable to a dedicated central government minister in the Cabinet (James Griffiths from 1964). It was a process that ended – despite the setback of a negative referendum outcome in 1979 (a pro-'British' move in some way ominously replicated in the pro-Brexit vote of 2016) – with the establishing in 1997 of a National Assembly for Wales (albeit with very limited powers) in Cardiff Bay. By this time, Wales was also served by its own national bodies over a very wide spectrum of areas, including culture, sport and publishing, and Cardiff had developed to become worthy of its status (since 1955) as the capital city of Wales.

Blodeuwedd

twentieth century

Hours too soon a barn owl
broke from woodshadow.
Her white face
rose out of darkness
in a buttercup field.

Colourless and soundless, feathers
cream as meadowsweet
and oakflowers, condemned
to the night, to lie alone
with her sin.

Deprived too of afternoons
in the comfortable sisterhood
of women moving in kitchens
among cups, cloths and running
water while they talk,

as we three talk tonight
in Hendre, the journey over.
We pare and measure and stir,
heap washed apples in a bowl, recall
the day's work, our own fidelities.

Her night lament
beyond conversation,
the owl follows
her shadow like a cross
over the fields,

Blodeuwedd's ballad
where the long reach
of the peninsula
is black in a sea
aghast with gazing.

One of the most haunting of the several wonderful tales to emerge from medieval Wales is that of Blodeuwedd. Fashioned from flowers to suit a husband's needs, she understandably rebelled against her preordained fate by proving unfaithful, for which her punishment was to be turned into an owl and to be condemned to dwell in everlasting darkness. The story has greatly appealed to the women writers of modern Wales who have refashioned it completely to reflect their own gradual emergence into the light. The sympathy of Gillian Clarke is therefore very evidently with the poor benighted Blodeuwedd of the original story, in whose condition she sees the imperfect state of liberation of women even in today's world.

Very little is known to us for the best part of two millennia of the history of women in Wales, but a few names do gleam defiantly even in that oppressive gloom. The twelfth-century Gwenllian is remembered as a woman of action, who undertook to lead a rebellious assault on the formidable Anglo-Norman fortress of Kidwelly in her husband's absence, only to be killed in the process. Catrin o Ferain supposedly had six husbands, killing five of them, and had so many descendants she was dubbed 'the Mother of Wales'. The figure of the beautiful Nest, the *femme fatale* of the late Middle Ages and the 'Helen of Wales', is still radioactive with glamour, as is that of Siwan (Joan), daughter of King John and wife of Llywelyn the Great, who briefly enjoyed a rebellious affair with William de Breos. The name Lleucu Llwyd remains brightly haloed with romance, thanks to the moving elegy dedicated to her in the fourteenth century by Llewelyn Goch ap Meurig Hen. But a dark fate awaited others of that time. Gwenllian, the daughter of Llywelyn the Last, ended her life in an English convent following his death, while Owain Glyndŵr's wife, Margaret, spent her last days banged up with her two daughters in the grim Tower of London. That rarity, a woman among the frequently laddish bards, the feisty fifteenth-century Gwerful Mechain remains memorable for her inventive, uninhibited riffs in joyous praise of her own sexual organs.

In the late eighteenth century, the interesting Madame Griffith enjoyed an intense relationship, of tantalisingly indeterminate character, with the great Methodist leader Howel Harris, while little Mary Jones became a folk heroine and effective founder of the British and Foreign Bible Society when she trekked barefoot some twenty-six miles to Bala in search of a Bible. Almost three hundred years ahead of *#MeToo*, the redoubtable boat-woman of Snowdonia, Margaret Evans, tipped the millionaire owner of the local quarry unceremoniously into a lake for making improper advances. Down in Fishguard, Jemima

Nicholas, her scarlet-skirted followers in their tall black hats resembling British Redcoats, fooled an invading French force into surrender at the sharp end of pitchforks.

In the next century, Augusta, the wife of 'Big Ben' (Sir Benjamin Hall, industrialist), loved to dress up in Welsh costume, and as the conspicuously gracious Lady Llanover she presided over a mini-renaissance of Welsh culture in the nineteenth century; while Charlotte Guest, wife of another industrialist, took Welsh legends to the world when she translated *The Mabinogion*. More intrepid, however, was Betsi Cadwaladr, a much more enlightened but less famous nurse in the Crimea than Florence Nightingale; while Cranogwen (Sarah Jane Rees) became the pioneering editor of the first magazine for women, but only after an astonishing first career as a Master Mariner.

The most colourful figure of all, though, was Amy Dillwyn, the flamboyantly cross-dressing and cigar-smoking daughter of an industrialist, who took over the managing of his spelter works on his death and was a leading Welsh figure in the struggle for female suffrage. A striking example of the educational advancement of highly talented women was Frances Hoggan (née Morgan), who became in 1870 the first British woman to receive a doctorate in medicine from any university in Europe. She later went on to an important international career promoting the education of women in all matters relating to their well-being, and demonstrating a particular interest in racial issues. Another arresting character was Eluned Morgan, born aboard a ship travelling from Britain to the Welsh settlement in Patagonia.

Sent home to Wales for education at Dolgellau, she developed into a notable writer who published a striking account of her epic journey from the original settlements on the East coast of Patagonia all the way to the later Welsh settlements at the foot of the Andes, the virtual breadth of a continent away in the far distant west.

The suffrage movement didn't really make much headway in Wales until the late nineteenth century, when several branches of the leading English societies advocating a vote for women were gradually established in the country, attracting very little support from the cockahoop male Liberal leadership. Winifred Coombe Tenant, wife of a prominent industrialist, campaigned vigorously for such a vote, and after the First World War became an important patron of talented young Welsh artists of working-class background. The chapels (exceedingly anxious in the face of the charge of moral laxity and lasciviousness laid against Welsh women in the notorious Blue Books report of 1847 to stress the moral rectitude of the female sex) generally confined them strictly to the supporting roles of dutiful wives and mothers.

It was an approach well suited to the demands of a new society centred on heavy industries, where in mines and before fiery furnaces men were required to bear the burden of extremely heavy labour. And, although some women had themselves at one time been employed in such work, it was the wives and families that often suffered most at times of hardship and of strike, and it was the men who were always in the limelight. As a 'worthy cause', the

Temperance Movement was one in which some middle-class Victorian women could be respectably involved. The working-class majority of them, however, were destined to be slowly worn down by interminable child-bearing, grindingly unavoidable domestic labour, and grief at the inevitable toll of child mortality. Among the top ten killers of children under five in Pontypridd in the last decade of Victoria's reign were pneumonia, fits, dysentery and measles, with the grisly diseases of whooping cough, diphtheria and scarlet fever following eagerly in the van.

The Great War gave women the first taste of doing men's work in Wales, as throughout Britain – those working in the many munitions factories were exposed to significant risks – but after the war they mostly resumed their former strictly subordinate stations. For many, living conditions at home were dreadful, with workers' houses in the Rhondda, for example, suffering from gross overcrowding. Unsanitary conditions meant that disease was often rife – in the 1930s, Lloyd George's daughter Megan, then a young MP for Anglesey, pointed out that there was a higher percentage of women suffering from tuberculosis in her constituency than almost anywhere else in Britain.

Yet women usually took great pride in being 'tidy' – respectable, in South Wales parlance – and came to be seen in almost mythic terms as the heart and soul of the family, a notion immortalised in the figure of the 'Welsh Mam'. As invisible as the crucial domestic contributions of wives and mothers was the hard life of the many young girls forced to seek work in London and elsewhere as

domestic help between the wars, some of whom were
sexually and otherwise abused. The 1920s, however,
did see a number of measures that significantly improved
women's situation, culminating in 1928 when women
were at last granted the same electoral rights as men.
A prominent role in campaigning for such a measure
was taken by the impressive feminist Margaret Haig
Thomas, Viscountess Rhondda. After the war, a generation
of young women were at long last provided with advanced
educational opportunities not only by the University of
Wales (the first female undergraduate admitted was
Louise Davies who, in 1884, entered the University
College of Wales, Aberystwyth, at the age of sixteen) but
also by the teacher training colleges whose contribution
to the educational scene in Wales has been scandalously
underestimated.

With the advent of post-industrialisation, and with
it all the other innovations that came with modernisation
(including, of course, the contraceptive pill that freed
women from the cruelly punishing fate of serial childbirth),
women began to take advantage of new freedoms and the
new opportunities for employment not just to supplement
family incomes but often to supply the income that was
no longer forthcoming through their menfolk. And when
what remained of the workforce of the mines went on
strike for what turned out to be the last time in 1984–5,
the militant women of the Valleys stood at the very public
forefront of the struggle. Meanwhile, the increasingly
mixed economy that powered the development of the

urban centres such
as Cardiff and Swansea
especially became very
dependent on a ready supply of female labour, while
both private businesses and the public, governmental
sector that grew dramatically in Wales after the war,
provided women with opportunities at every grade and
level, including at the very top. By the time a National
Assembly was established in 1997, it seemed natural for
it to adopt a policy both of ensuring that at least half its
members were female, and of arranging that sessions
would be limited to family-friendly hours – one of several
progressive measures it introduced over the next twenty
years, including the establishing of a Youth Assembly.

MENNA ELFYN

Siapau o Gymru
The shapes she makes
twenty-first century

Ei diffinio rown
ar fwrdd glân,
rhoi ffurf i'w ffiniau,
ei gyrru i'w gororau
mewn inc coch;
ac meddai myfyriwr o bant,
'*It's like a pig running away*';
wedi bennu chwerthin,
rwy'n ei chredu;
y swch gogleddol
yn heglu'n gynt
na'r swrn deheuol
ar ffo rhag y lladdwyr.

Siapau yw hi siŵr iawn:

yr hen geg hanner rhwth
neu'r fraich laes ddiog
sy'n gorffwys ar ei rhwyfau;
y jwmpwr, wrth gwrs,
        ar ei hanner,
gweill a darn o bellen ynddi,
ynteu'n debyg i siswrn
parod i'w ddarnio'i hun;
cyllell ddeucarn anturiaethydd,
neu biser o bridd
craciedig a gwag.

A lluniau amlsillafog
yw'r tirbeth o droeon
a ffeiriaf â'm cydnabod
a chyda'r estron
sy'n ei gweld am yr hyn yw:
ddigri o wasgaredig
sy
am
fy
mywyd
        fel bwmarang diffael yn mynnu
                        mynnu
                ffendio'i
            ffordd
        yn ôl
    at
fy nhraed.

I was defining her
on a clean slate,
fleshing out her frontiers,
badgering out her borders
in red ink;
when a foreign student said
'it's like a pig running away';
laughing done with,
I believe her;
the northern snout
hoofing it faster
than her southern rump,
fleeing her slaughterers.

She's made of shapes, you know;

the slack old mouth, agape
or the lazy, lolling arm,
resting on its oars;
the jumper, of course,
    half-done;
wrapped around a bit of wool and the needles,
or else, she's a pair of scissors
ready to ribbon herself,
an adventurer's double-hafted knife,
or an earthen pitcher,
hollow and cracked.

She's polysyllabled pictures.
this inleted landmass
I swap with acquaintances
and with the foreigner
who sees her for what she is:
comically scattered
who is,
on my life,
    like an unerring boomerang which wills
             wills
         its
      way
    back
  to
my
feet.

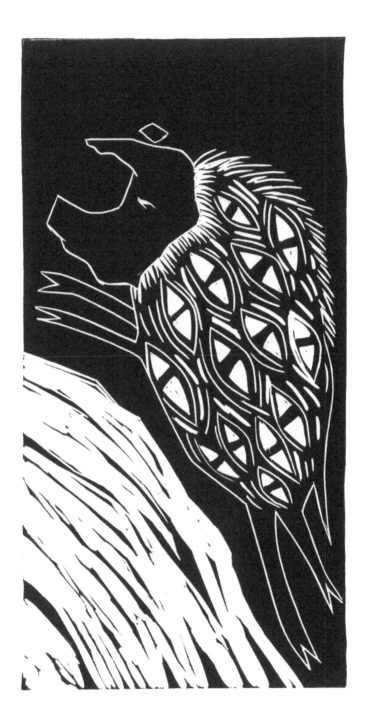

The post-industrial story of Wales since 1945 seems, in one way, still to be work-in-progress, far too amorphous and multifaceted to be filed tidily away under neat stereotypes and generalisations. The Wales that is emerging is a strange country, constantly changing shape in myriad weirdly and wonderfully unpredictable ways. But yet, in another sense it all seems strangely familiar. Wales remains a chronically dependent country, still uncertain whether it is a region of Anglo-Britain or a 'nation' in its own right: prevarication seems to be the default condition of this tease of a people – a legacy perhaps of long centuries of ducking and weaving. It still has no control over its own economy, that great determinant of every aspect of life.

It remains what it has been for most of its history – locked inexorably in survival mode, whether its cultural life of choice be lived through the medium of English or of Welsh. Accordingly, this tiny country (yet still twice the population of Estonia, bigger than Latvia and Slovenia, the same size as Lithuania, and only marginally smaller than Ireland and New Zealand) has to resort to ceaseless improvisation and cunning adaptation on all fronts.

It has returned to being one of the most backward and impoverished regions of Britain and spends most of its time playing catch-up best it can – Wales managed to gain a degree of control over its broadcast media only after long decades of struggle, and now finds itself similarly disadvantaged in the new, digital age.

Communication continues to be a chronic problem. There are still no convenient routes linking South Wales to North Wales, with the latter region orientating itself towards Liverpool and the former – for all the welcome vibrancy of the 'new Cardiff' – increasingly leaning, via Newport, towards Bristol. East-west motorway development eases travel greatly, but the M4, a vital artery of trade, is a mixed blessing: greatly facilitating both inward investment and export, it helps attract newcomers to refresh and reinvigorate local society, but mass migration (in both directions) brings consequences in its train that are difficult either to calibrate or to manage. Wales haemorrhages talent to England at an alarming rate. The long, slow decline of rural areas continues, only now to find itself unnervingly mirrored in the decline of the erstwhile great centres of industry. The Welsh media industry is in a state of turmoil and crisis, and the underfunded and overmanaged HE system lags well behind those of England, Scotland and Northern Ireland. Occasional, welcome, examples of sporting success aside, strong markers of separate identity seem one by one to be getting weaker.

And even though Wales had, with a last defiant

flourish of the old solidarities of industrial society, fiercely
rejected Thatcher (most heroically in the obdurate strike
of 1984–5, the miners' last stand), the young of today
still seem very much Thatcher's children, if unwittingly so.
For them, it often seems, there is no such thing as society –
or at least a Welsh society to which they feel they owe any
allegiance. For all the patiently corrective and enlightened
social policies of the Welsh government at its best, Anglo-
American culture serenely rules the roost. As for the relaxed
pluralism of the age, it is obviously to be highly valued in
many respects, not least for its tolerance of ethnic as well
as gender difference (even if Trevor Fishlock's generous
view that xenophobia is a comparative rarity in Wales
is sadly questionable), but it poses obvious difficulties
(although also no doubt many new opportunities) for the
maintenance of any precarious 'local' collectivity. Jan Morris
once pithily suggested that being Welsh means being
afflicted by old torments reminiscent of a Celtic fairy-tale.
The Torment of the Confused Identity; the Torment of the
Torn Tongue; and the Torment of the Two Peoples – one
bilingual, the other monoglot English speakers.

Given all these challenges to continued survival, it is
one of the very minor wonders of the modern world that
a Wales still exists. 'Rŷn ni yma o hyd'/ 'We are still here,'
as Dafydd Iwan's celebrated popular song has it – if only
just, as Welshness seems to be becoming ever more a
matter of sentiment (the seven Triple Crowns of the rugby
team in the late 1960s and 1970s, and Wales's unlikely
success in the soccer Euros of 2016 being heady examples,

along with Geraint Thomas's 2018 victory at the Tour de France) than of substance. As for the sentiment, it may by now be little more than what Freud scathingly termed 'the narcissism of minor difference'.

But then, the people of Wales are long used to reshaping their land and reviewing their identity, as Menna Elfyn's poem makes clear. Indeed, the single most persistent and distinctive identifying feature of the Welsh people, from their beginning way back in the time of Catraeth to the present, has been their mute, inexplicable, unbreakable determination to survive – and to survive in whatever form and under whatever circumstances might be dictated by situations that, after all, have almost always been out of their own control. Long may that gloriously perverse determination continue.